Extreme Engineering

GOLDEN GATE BRIDGE

BY TERA KELLEY

WWW.APEXEDITIONS.COM

Copyright © 2024 by Apex Editions, Mendota Heights, MN 55120. All rights reserved. No part of this book may be reproduced or utilized in any form or by any means without written permission from the publisher.

Apex is distributed by North Star Editions:
sales@northstareditions.com | 888-417-0195

Produced for Apex by Red Line Editorial.

Photographs ©: Shutterstock Images, cover, 1, 4–5, 6–7, 8, 12–13, 15, 22–23, 24, 25, 26, 29; Library of Congress, 10–11; Chas. M. Hiller/Library of Congress, 16–17; Historic Illustrations/Alamy, 18; AP Images, 19; Underwood Archives, Inc/Alamy, 20–21; Paul Chinn/San Francisco Chronicle/AP Images, 27

Library of Congress Control Number: 2023910818

ISBN
978-1-63738-749-8 (hardcover)
978-1-63738-792-4 (paperback)
978-1-63738-876-1 (ebook pdf)
978-1-63738-835-8 (hosted ebook)

Printed in the United States of America
Mankato, MN
012024

NOTE TO PARENTS AND EDUCATORS

Apex books are designed to build literacy skills in striving readers. Exciting, high-interest content attracts and holds readers' attention. The text is carefully leveled to allow students to achieve success quickly. Additional features, such as bolded glossary words for difficult terms, help build comprehension.

CHAPTER 1
THROUGH THE FOG 4

CHAPTER 2
WHY IT WAS BUILT 10

CHAPTER 3
CONSTRUCTION 16

CHAPTER 4
GRAND OPENING 22

COMPREHENSION QUESTIONS • 28
GLOSSARY • 30
TO LEARN MORE • 31
ABOUT THE AUTHOR • 31
INDEX • 32

CHAPTER 1

THROUGH THE FOG

A family drives to San Francisco, California. To get there, they cross the Golden Gate Bridge.

San Francisco is in Northern California. It is one of the largest cities in the state.

Fog covers most of the bridge. But two towers stick out through the clouds. Each tower is 746 feet (227 m) tall.

San Francisco is known for its heavy fog.

WHY ORANGE?

The Golden Gate Bridge is not actually painted gold. The builders chose a reddish-orange color. This color stands out against the fog. It is called **international** orange.

Thick cables curve down from the towers. The family drives between them on a long roadway. They see San Francisco Bay on the east side of the bridge.

FAST FACT

The Golden Gate Bridge is 1.7 miles (2.7 km) long. The road is more than 200 feet (60 m) above the water.

As of 2023, the cables that hold up the bridge were the largest bridge cables ever made.

CHAPTER 2

Why It Was Built

San Francisco was built near a bay. The bay connects to a **strait** called the Golden Gate. For many years, the strait could only be crossed on a **ferry**.

Much of San Francisco Bay is shallow. But it is more than 300 feet (90 m) deep at the Golden Gate.

The strong winds in San Francisco Bay make it good for sailing.

Many people agreed that they needed a bridge. But the strait was very wide. It also had dangerous winds.

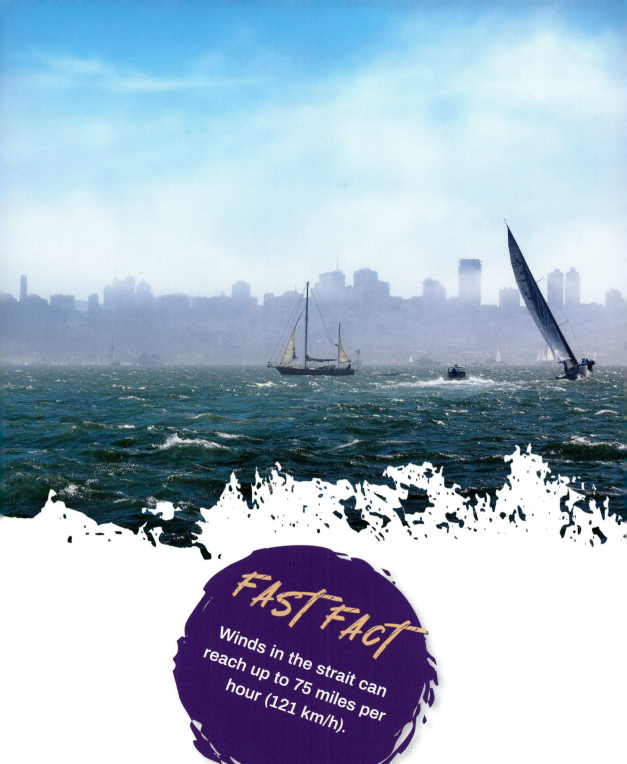

FAST FACT

Winds in the strait can reach up to 75 miles per hour (121 km/h).

By 1929, **engineers** decided to build a **suspension bridge**. Strong cables would hold up the bridge. This new **design** allowed it to cross the strait.

BAD IDEA

The engineers' first idea was a hybrid bridge. It used parts of old bridge designs. But it also used new ideas. The engineers decided it was too ugly.

Joseph Strauss helped design the Golden Gate Bridge. His statue stands nearby.

CHAPTER 3

First, the bridge needed a strong **foundation** on each side of the strait. Then, workers built the towers. The north tower went on land.

Construction of the Golden Gate Bridge began in 1933.

Workers pumped more than 9 million gallons (34 million L) of water out of the oval. This made space for the foundation.

On the south side, workers built an oval wall in the water. That way, they could build a foundation in the strait. The south tower went on top. Next, workers ran the main cables over both towers.

FAST FACT

Each main cable of the bridge is about 3 feet (0.9 m) thick.

The main cables were made by pressing thousands of thin wires together.

On suspension bridges, towers hold up the roadway. The cables allow the towers to carry the weight.

The main cables were attached to each end of the bridge. Then, workers hung 500 smaller cables from the main cables. The ends were attached to the roadway.

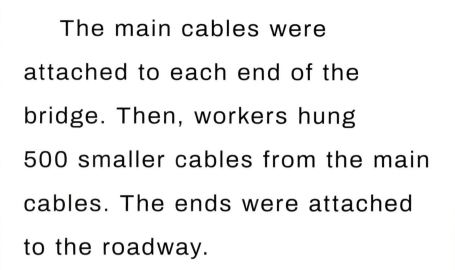

SIDEWAYS SWAY

The cables let the roadway move. It can sway nearly 28 feet (8.5 m) from side to side. That helps the bridge stay up when there are strong winds.

CHAPTER 4

GRAND OPENING

The Golden Gate Bridge opened on May 27, 1937. For nearly 30 years, it was the longest suspension bridge in the world.

At the time the bridge was completed, it had the tallest bridge towers in the world.

More than 30 painters work to keep the Golden Gate Bridge from rusting.

The bridge became famous for its simple but beautiful design. People loved its elegant shape and bright color.

REPAIRS

Workers repaint parts of the bridge often. That helps protect it from rust. **Ironworkers** also work on the bridge. They replace old parts, such as bolts and rivets.

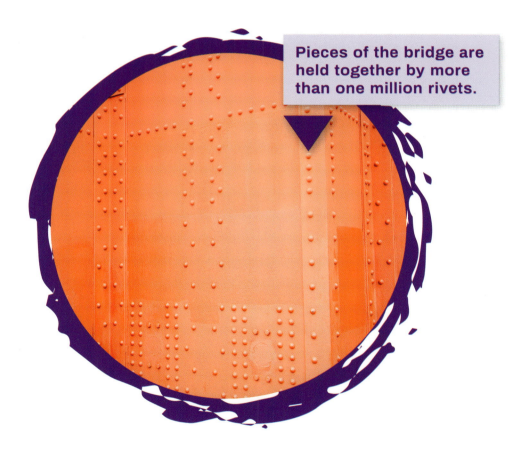

Pieces of the bridge are held together by more than one million rivets.

People pay to drive across the bridge. In the early 2020s, more than 100,000 cars crossed it every day.

People can walk across the bridge for free.

FAST FACT
In 2015, a Moveable Median Barrier was built on the bridge. It adds or removes lanes during busy times.

The Moveable Median Barrier uses a special truck to move concrete blocks. It takes about 30 minutes.

COMPREHENSION QUESTIONS

Write your answers on a separate piece of paper.

1. Write a few sentences describing how workers built the Golden Gate Bridge.

2. Which part of the Golden Gate Bridge do you think is most interesting? Why?

3. How long is the Golden Gate Bridge?
    - A. 300 feet (90 m)
    - B. 746 feet (227 m)
    - C. 1.7 miles (2.7 km)

4. Why might it be important for the bridge to stand out against the fog?
    - A. so boats can see the bridge and steer around it
    - B. so people can see the bridge from space
    - C. because bright colors of paint cost less

5. What does **hybrid** mean in this book?

*The engineers' first idea was a **hybrid** bridge. It used parts of old bridge designs. But it also used new ideas.*

    A. made by using extra-strong materials
    B. made by combining two different things
    C. made by reusing parts of buildings

6. What does **elegant** mean in this book?

*The bridge became famous for its simple but beautiful design. People loved its **elegant** shape and bright color.*

    A. ugly or unoriginal
    B. extremely tall and wide
    C. well-made and nice to look at

Answer key on page 32.

GLOSSARY

design
A plan for how to make or build something.

engineers
People who use math and science to solve problems.

ferry
A boat that transports people and cars across water.

foundation
The lowest part of a structure, often made below ground level.

international
Having to do with many countries.

ironworkers
People who build structures or parts with iron.

strait
A narrow passage of water that connects two larger bodies of water.

suspension bridge
A bridge that is supported by small cables attached to larger cables that run between towers.

BOOKS

Bowman, Chris. *Bridges*. Minneapolis: Bellwether Media, 2019.

Dittmer, Lori. *Golden Gate Bridge*. Mankato, MN: Creative Education, 2019.

Morrow, Kate. *Building a Bridge*. Mendota Heights, MN: Focus Readers, 2020.

ONLINE RESOURCES

Visit **www.apexeditions.com** to find links and resources related to this title.

ABOUT THE AUTHOR

Tera Kelley is the author of *Listen to the Language of the Trees*, an NPR 2022 Books We Love selection and a Blueberry Award winner. She lives 20 minutes from the Golden Gate Bridge.

C
cables, 9, 14, 18–19, 21

F
ferry, 10
fog, 6–7
foundation, 16, 18

G
Golden Gate, 10

P
paint, 7, 25

R
roadway, 9, 21
rust, 25

S
San Francisco, California, 4, 10
San Francisco Bay, 9, 10
strait, 10, 12–14, 16, 18
suspension bridge, 14, 22

T
towers, 6, 9, 16, 18

W
winds, 12–13, 21

ANSWER KEY:
1. Answers will vary; 2. Answers will vary; 3. C; 4. A; 5. B; 6. C